Breathing in Beauty

Uplifting Poems and Inspiring Sayings
A Journey of Self-Awakening

Barbara Lager

CREATOPIA
An imprint of Tesseray Publishing

Book and Cover Design: Monette Satterfield

Fonts: Bitter and Great Vibes

Author Photo: Dawn Vogel

ISBN: 978-1-961912-02-1
Library of Congress Control Number: 2023948177

Published by Creatopia®, an imprint of Tesseray Publishing LLC
7635 148th Street West, #329
Apple Valley, MN 55124
www.TesserayPublishing.com

Dedication

I'm dedicating this book to my extraordinary
mother Mae Velen who not only showed me
love but exemplified the most positive spirit.
Mae was loved by all who knew her.

I'm also dedicating this book to my beautiful
husband Daniel Lager for your constant love
and support throughout all our adventurous
years together,
 I love you!

Along with my two amazing sons, Nick Larner
and Parker Lager, you always make me so
proud to be your mother. I love you both more
than there are stars in the universe.

Contents

iii

Forward

Barbara Lager is a Mystic Poet - she sees with the expansive vision of eyes of the heart. As a writer and receiver of ecstatic poetry, she is a wise and an open-hearted person, one of my dearest friends and gratefully my first cousin, a soul champion to me throughout my life. I have also been deeply inspired as a longtime Yoga and Meditation Teacher by the themes and wisdom in her poetry and inspirational sayings.

Barbara's writing has been curated throughout most of her life with a contemplative writing practice. She now has offered us this generous book "Breathing in Beauty" of spirit wisdom coming through clearly, a divine messenger of imagery inspired words that take us into deep truths, compassion, and self-love. Barbara's words speak to the natural abundance of our souls in a visual language that both holds and expands our being.

Poetry that is both earthy and boundless!

You will find that no matter where you open the book on a given day, Barbara's words offer pure balm and soul medicine.

I have swum in the glorious beauty of Barbara's poetry and inspirational sayings and benefited greatly over the years. I trust that for those that have ears to hear, and need for these magical truths, that they have arrived at the perfect time. I have incredible happiness knowing others will be inspired on their mystic and spiritual path reading "Breathing in Beauty."

Wendy Lindahl M.A., Body and Soul Wisdom
Wellness Facilitator
Sedona, Arizona

Preface

"Breathing in Beauty" is a collection of poems and inspirational sayings that reflect my positive, creative and loving nature, mixed in with soft bursts of pure higher wisdom, as well as my insights from moments of deep contemplation. These writings are the result of my ongoing journey of awakening to the joy and fulfillment of self-belonging. Soul Diving into the question of what it feels like to be fully alive with an unbridled passion for life, and to be authentically connected to myself and others.

I wrote many of these poems in the mornings, with a cup of coffee in hand, gazing out the window at the treetops and the vastness of the sky. Sometimes I wrote on my deck, taking in life in motion, or while walking in nature.

Writing has always been my constant, closest companion and teacher, as I continue to ask the questions in search of the answers. My answers have become a ripple of love in this world, and I call it "Breathing in Beauty."

I feel blessed to share my poems and sayings with you, hoping that they will become their own unique ripples of love in your life. As you read my poetry and sayings, I hope that you feel as though you are breathing in beauty. To touch another's heart is a true gift, and for this I am deeply grateful.

Blessings,
Barbara Lager

Essence

Creativity is the perfume of the Universe...

With its scent
it awakens others.

We each carry with us,
our own unique fragrance.

What gifts await me today?

A New Day

The day pours open
"Come inside," it whispers,
"Bring to me your Body, Mind, and Spirit.
Come play with me -
I will show you things
you never even thought you could imagine."

Sunlight leads me in,
like the hand of a familiar lover.
With grace and ease I freely follow.
I stand in the newness of the promise of today,
excited to BE.

Making way for anything to come.
Every moment of today,
I will cherish.
I give to it my unbounded passion.

Tonight, as I lay my head upon my pillow
under the luminous stars,
I will blanket my heart up,
with all the exquisite memories
that this New Day has brought to me.

The only thing that I will direct today, is the direction of my smile.

Sweet Spirit of Life

I look to the future,
beautiful fragments of light lay on my path,
leading me towards a new direction to go.

Stillness is my companion,
along my way...

I breathe in peace.
I am ever so grateful for this bridge of love,
that creates a way for my soul to go.

Sweet Spirit of Life-
I pour myself open, amongst humanity;
Sweet Spirit of Love- that endures time.

You will be my legacy.
Plant a tree for me,
watch it take root.
Learn from its roots,
plant yourself in love and joy.

Peace for all.

Never doubt your strength,
your unique beauty.
Grow toward what speaks to your spirit.
Become strong, in your message of love.

Sweet Spirit of Life.

Treasures

You don't have to give me something beautiful,
show me that I am beautiful with your eyes.

You don't have to impress me with how much you
know,
show me how much that you care.

These are my most cherished treasures,
the ones that cannot be sold.

I will hold them close to my soul, ever so tight.
These will be the ones I guard, with all my might.

At the end of each day I will smile,
as I say goodnight.

Friendships are the colorful threads of life...
They create a delicate tapestry that decorates
our hearts.

The Gift

I smelled your Love

on

the

bouquet

of

flowers

you gave me

today.

Relax into the beauty of this world.

Feather Magic

Hope is as light as a feather
as it wisps weightlessly pass my heart
and tickles my soul.

Feather Magic with its lightness of being;
Like eyelash kisses, giggling with pleasure.
The sweetness of its memory –
lingers on in my Mind's Eye.
Just thinking of it
brings me lightness, where there was once
darkness.

I smile ever so tenderly,
so fragile - like my spirit.
I am not so strong at times,
small memories give me great hope.
There is great strength in places so fragile.

I will look for the light everywhere;
Feather Magic.

Be kind to yourself, and the world will be kind to you.

Guardian of Light

She spoke to my soul...
an invitation to rest in her light.

Bathed in tranquility, by her presence.
Awakened by her softness, her kindness.

"Gentle soul" she spoke to me,
no words were even necessary.

Enraptured in the celebration of this light,
so beautiful our being together.

The fragrance of this gathering smells like
Bliss,
as it lingers in the air.

I know that;

I am blessed
I am seen
I am heard
I am felt
I feel
It is so
I AM so.

Grateful for this joy
which has led me here to this secret meeting
place
with my Guardian of Light.

She flies away, never far.

Leaving the essence of her light;
 for me to use,
 depend upon,
 follow and celebrate.
 This sacred elixir of Love.

Seed of My Being

I experienced the splendor of this day,
folding into itself,
as the day slowly unfolds.

Reaching inside for my inner joy,
awakens my senses.

Nestled in the fertile soil of me
rests the seed of my being.
Convening with my nature,
as it cultivates my self-kindness.

Rooted deeply in my eyes,
this is why and how I see things.

Wisdom's light nourishes this seed
helping me to grow strong and flourish
with its astonishing presence
the Seed of My Being.

I feed my soul with delight...
Great things grow from there.

Becoming

Who am I becoming
a part of me already exists,
while other parts are waiting to be conceived,
in the womb of my spirit.
New elements spring forth from this portal of
my being,
as they breathe outside of my body now.

SELF- judgment d i s a p p e a r s

As this constant lover of life yearns so deeply
inside of me.
This fragile side of me, is being ever so
nurtured by my inner child.
Eagerly, falling forward softly as I take my
place,
humbled by my vulnerability.

Becoming... more myself everyday

healthy - whole - strong - forgiving - patient

I AM forever blessed in this world,
graced by my visions of love
always looking for signs from the Universe
to lead me on my path of who I AM,
Becoming...

Be the One

I must be the one to navigate my way,
a way, throughout my life.
If not me, I ask...
then who?

Activating new ways into my sense of wonderment.
New stories free me from old stories that sometimes
felt like quicksand along my way.

Wide open am I...

I must be the one, leading me towards vast
undiscovered destinations.
Doorways opening into others' hearts,
as other doors close.
Beauty, grace and awe mark my way.
Self-connectedness leads me on this journey,
always closer to myself, and to others.
Wherever this exquisite journey shall take me,
I must be MY one.

Today my life is expanding, in exquisite and meaningful ways.

Language of Love

Today I speak the Language of Love-
with all beings and creatures.
I find our language,
OUR native tongue.
Language which is indigenous to all.

Language of Love-
no words,
few,
some,
many.

This language we are born from and reborn,
cultivated in the heart space of our authentic being.
This language, which sparks and speaks to the
Universe.

Language of Love-

Always resting on our tongues, in our eyes, our
bodies, our spirits.
Coming alive in our yearning.
So easily awakened
and eager to speak.

Hungry to hear,
feel,
and
touch.
This is the Language of Love.

Inner Peace

This quiet,
this beauty,
this thing that I yearn for,
 is here for me now.

Stay for a while,
let me bathe in your presence.
Allow me to linger in your authentic beauty.
Be touched by your wisdom again, old friend.

Like an old friend who slips into my life
without warning.
So happy to see, feel and touch.
Ecstatic to be in the company of you.

Stay as you wish...

Leave the door to my soul open,
For when you arrive back again.

Beautiful day...Bring me your light.

I Hear it Saying

Spirit whispering, "*Rest...*

I will be your medicine,
you don't have to do a thing.
I love you... just the way you are
nothing is required of you.
Bask in this quietude of my gift.
You are so beautiful.
Breathe in, breathe out,
delight in the movement of your chest."

How many breaths will make up this lifetime...
My first breath taking hold of life, never stopping
until my final breath.
Where will I go...
As I follow each breath upon my journey.
The highs and lows of life replicating my own
body's rhythmic patterns of breathing.

My journey's unfolding
is similar to that of the petals of a flower,
colorful, fragrant and uniquely delicate all
existing at the same time.

I am awakened by the magic that speaks to my soul.

Spiritual Essence

Peace
came
and
led
me
into the silence.

It is there
I
found
my largest spaces.

Defined
in the eyes of my
stillness...

I walk through everything, to find myself.

Stardust

Stardust from which we are all created,
the light that shimmers,
as we shine.

Bearing witness
to our passions, as they are revealed.

Lighting up
making way for others to explode in their
Stardust.

I push off towards the direction of my dreams.

Flying High

New beats sound off to the pulse of my life today.
Each beat seems to be dipped in the essence of joy,
as it is softly serenaded by the rhythm of my heart
beating.

I am astounded by the way my inner landscape has
become enlivened again.
Rejoicing in my birthright.

I am free to explore new heights of the land of my
existence.
Courage is as natural as breathing with this fresh
paradigm.
I begin moving forward,
as I soar higher.
Celebrating the magical view of flying high once again.

Open hearts, fly the highest...

Morning

In the morning
I strike the match
which lights the flame
that sparks the light
that lies
inside of me.

Igniting
my
inner flame
with
visions
of
possibilities.

Giving me reasons
to
live
my
day.

I walk into the light...

I am able to see clearly now.

Day by Day

I AM enraptured by grace...
A vessel of love
delivered by source.

The seed was planted upon my arrival, the one
that I grow from.

The depth of my presence has no platform,
from which I stand.

I am surrounded only by my thoughts, which
holds me up.

All the beauty in my world...

Rests in my heart.

After the Storm

See what glimmers inside,
what gifts have I cultivated
after the storm... in my Spirit.
What wisdom shimmers with all of its glory.
I do not need to guard this prized possession,
I will wear it boldly.

MY RESILIENCE rising up again...
To breathe
to be
to love
to laugh
to play
to cry
to try again.
This marvelous gift called LIFE.

Contrast allows my beauty to shine... even brighter.

White Light

There is a sacred place inside of me...

Where all roads intersect, inside my mystical
sanctuary.

Housing my White Light.

White Light spreads its luminous gifts throughout.

Creasing open the air, taking only the space that is
needed.

Creating my place to be.
Giving so generously of its expression of
undeniable truths.

White Light speaks with a language all of its own.

Penetrating into my depths, my never fading
White Light.

My light has awakened my soul...
It is there I find my treasures.

Being

I do not know you,
    by the color of your skin.

I do not judge you,
    by false lines in the sand.

I do not measure your character,
    by the amount of currency in your bank
account.

I know you by your intrinsic light that you shine.

By the way your eyes smile at me, feeling like
home,
    leading me closer to who you are.

The ripple of your love in this world, that sends out
the message,
    we are no different.

You and I are beautiful emanations of magnificent blessings.

Our connection exists in being alive.

Intimate in breath, hearts beating, craving to BE.

We do not move in the same direction.

We follow our own way, walking on our unique pathway.

Sometimes alone...

Sometimes together...

Sometimes simply just by being.

Drinking in Love

Today, I drank in Love...
Love's sweet nectar fed my soul.

As it filled up my vessel, till it was spilling over.

Kindness is my compass,
for the way in which I turn my intentions.

Compassion is the road I walk down.

Miracles are in my life, my every thought.

I walk with my family.

God my Father,
Nature my Mother.

Today... I follow my dreams, and see where they take me.

Soaring

I let go of everything and held on to love.

As I spread my wings soaring to magical places
of my heart,
on warm breezes of sweet whispers.

Where our footprints have never been laid
before.

Come...
Hold on, look into my eyes my beloved.

Listen...
To the truth of (y)our passion.

Yearning together for the alchemy of this love.

Drown me in sacred joy...
I will find my breath.

Moonbeams

We are all Moonbeams-
radiating light upon our world.
Lighting up ourselves;
and each other along our way.
We stroll along in our brilliance, always longing
to spark a genuine connection.
Be courageous on your path.
Bathe yourself in your own miracles.
Shine your soul's dazzling light.
Be your own dance partner.
Make love to your mind,
and only then see where your pathway brings
you
and
to whom.

Who are you when you are rooted in your divine nature?

Tasty Morsels

Under the canopy of delight, I place myself.
Here is where I inhale deeply...

As I exhale joy... which permeates under my skin.
It's astounding nature feels ever so vibrant,
as it courses throughout my being.

I am filled up, as I allow myself to receive this gift.
All that I desire is this offering.
My insatiable craving yearns for this delectable
feast.

I eat it up, with all of me.
My voracious appetite is satisfied.
Here I lay at peace... that shows itself in the fullness
of that which I AM.

Joy is my compass...
Self-Love is my strength.

Moments in Time

Today...
I sprinkle my sweetness all over, under, inside
and out.
I ask the questions,
I repeat the phrases,
I live my truth.

I explode in the wonder of life.
I implode in the nature of my ego.

I relish these moments,
that I know everything is going to be alright.
I collapse with pleasure,
from this tug of my heart string.

I reach out for my world, and my world reaches back for me.

Heaven

I live my life looking for the beauty in my
world...
Falling in love with it.

Love being the closest thing to heaven.
Heaven on Earth
the more that I am able to love,
give and receive,
the closer
I am to heaven.

The voice of source conveys its messages of love...

It's the only voice that matters to me today.

I AM

I AM darkness, vastness of depth.
I AM light, boundless of infinite space.
I AM circles of my endless thoughts.
I AM playful with freedom.
I AM the ropes that bind me.
I AM the connectedness of love.
I AM the gathering of me.
I AM enough,
no one ever said I was not.

Who is this beauty that resides inside of me,
my constant companion in this lifetime.
Come out and play I say,
as the moonbeams awakened the softhearted
parts of me.
I dance alone in the moonlight,
in the garden of pure delight.
My feet are planted on the ground.
Mother Earth below,
Father Sky above.
Here is where I belong,
I AM...

Fragments

Millions of fragments of thoughts will have found
their way into the stream of my consciousness.
Mysteriously floating towards my
psyche, approaching in fleeting moments.
Each small piece will have claimed its place in
shaping me
who I once was,
who I AM
and
who I AM to become.

All leaving their unique remnants along the way.

SoulPrints embedded in my actions of lessons
learned.

Fragments cast their shadows, as some arrive
radiating their dazzling delight.

Equally important is the discovery of their contrast;

dark into light,

sorrow into hope,

indifference into connectedness.

Wisdom's key arrives for me,

I examine it with moments of contemplation of hope,

as I turn it into the doorway of my future.

Tapestry

I heard words today that wove my thoughts
together.

Words dancing and some stomping around

leaving their footprints upon my mind's eye to
ponder.

    spirit,

                mind,

                              body,

start to move in so many various directions at
once, without even taking one step.

Today, like everyday I hear words...

Some seem to have uncaged themselves from
my darkest places

brought into the light...

to be spoken, shared and witnessed.

Today, I heard the words that wove me
together and apart again.

Blessings

I take the hand of the Divine,
the hand I trust.

I move forward with certainty,
into uncertainty
awaiting my blessings
to arrive...

Beneath my surface, I hear a sacred voice
whispering, "Hi Beautiful."

Born

Born in love,
found in love,
lost in love...
I found my way home again.
Back to the quietness of my center,
where every crevice of my nature rests in this
calmness.
It's soothing sensation washes over all of me,
cleansing off and restoring me once again.

Born in love,
lost in love,
found in love...

My soul has awakened countless times,

through the eyes of love.

Traveler

Here I sit upon higher ground waiting.

Signs of her sheer divine presence swirling around me as luminous streaks.

She makes her way closer to me.

Closer than close.

She's here, in-between my spaces, I sigh with pure serenity.

Ever so lightly she knocks on the door of my soul.

I am comforted by the rhythm of her knocking.

Welcoming her eagerly, into the beauty of my land.

She ignites magical occurrences immediately
upon her arrival .

My words sprout out like fragrant flowers,
creating my sacred bouquet.

There we dance amongst the colorful petals
that cover the floor of my land.

Love

Use up all my love,
take every last drop.

Infuse me amongst humankind
and
only
then
I will know
I was here for my life's purpose.

I let go of everything, and hold on to love.

Altar

Today, I met myself at the sacred altar;
bridging the connection
between my inside and out.

Sculpting myself
as a vessel of peace,
as my words poured out.

Believe in Beauty

About Barbara Lager

Barbara Lager is a poet and artist born and raised in the vibrant city of Chicago, where she earned her bachelor's degree. Her poetry reflects her deep connection to the spiritual side of life, as she weaves her thoughts and words into inspiring and expressive verses. Writing poetry has been a natural and effortless outlet for her, bringing her poems to life on the pages.

She has also enjoyed traveling across the United States for over three decades, selling her unique and whimsical mixed-metal jewelry. She loves creating art and seeing the joy it brings to others, which has been a true blessing for her. All her creative endeavors are a bridge of love and pure passion for her soul to walk home.

She lives in St. Paul, MN with her wonderful husband Daniel and their children Nick, Parker, stepdaughter Jessica, son-in-law Adam, and grandchildren Colton and Cameron.

Acknowledgments

Acknowledgments to these wonderful people:
Nicole Fendi, my publisher, for opening the
door to this unforgettable journey; Monette
Satterfield, my outstanding editor, for your
wisdom; Cathy Cowen, my friend who said,
"There is a place in this world for your poetry;"
and Wendy Lindahl, my cousin, and soul diving
playmate.
Thank you all for the ways in which you have
been with me.

Thoughts

Thoughts

Printed in the USA
CPSIA information can be obtained
at www.ICGtesting.com
CBHW042131211023
1439CB00006B/11

9 781961 912021